INTRODUCTION TO THE SOUTH, OR HOW TO SUCCEED IN DIXIE WITHOUT EVEN CRYING

Bluffing can be a chancy business. It's often filled with pitfalls and pratfalls if you don't mind your step and guard your posterior every inch of the way. But in the case of the Deep South, you're in high cotton. That is to say, the sweet smell of magnolias, the flavor of ambrosia with fresh coconut cake, and the pungent chill of mint juleps will quickly convince the neophyte bluffer that this is *the* place to be—God's country. Don't worry, you'll do fine.

The "Deep South," like any world-famed "the," is a nebulous term, which dolts and dullards insist on applying to the most abject of states—particularly Kentucky, Maryland, and West Virginia. The term properly applies to the southern heartland—that is, Virginia, the Carolinas, Tennessee, Georgia, Alabama, Mississippi, Arkansas, East Texas, and Louisiana—the core of unreconstructed anti-Yankeedom and the home of molasses, jasmine, chicken-fried steak, the Dallas Cowboys cheerleaders, Louis Armstrong, Orville Faubus, Moon Pies, chow-chow, Dr. Pepper, and Uncle Remus.

Before you embark, however, shore up your peripheral knowledge of as many aspects of the South—deep *or* shallow—as you can muster. Pack this little treasure-trove in your old kitbag and smile, smile, smile. Start thinking in terms of "family" because successful bluffing means that you'll be accepted as "family."

A Quick Quiz, or Twenty Questions to Better Bluffery

Bone up on minutiae from below the Mason-Dixon with the following pop quiz. Score twenty points or more and you're a true Dixie Darlin'. Fifteen points is a fair showing, but requires at least a year's subscription to *Southern Living*. A score of ten is troubled waters; you need to eat lots more grits and see *Gone with the Wind* at least three more times. Five points means that you'd better pack your carpetbag and head back north on Amtrak. You're truly hopeless.

(1) What gentleman and scholar of Southern manhood graciously rendered up the sword of Southern military might at the Appomattox Court House on April 9, 1865?

(General Robert Edward Lee, alas. Score one extra point if you know what he did for a living after the war: served as president of Washington and Lee College.)

(2) Who valiantly led the Confederate army against General Hooker at Chancellorsville and died with a prayer for the South on his dedicated lips?

(General Thomas Jonathan "Stonewall" Jackson. Score one extra point if you know how he died: accidentally shot in the arm by one of his own men.)

(3) What two men headed up the Confederacy from their headquarters in Richmond?

(President Jefferson Davis and Vice President Alexander Hamilton Stephens. Subtract three points if you guessed John C. Calhoun.)

(4) What illustrious Virginia holiday honors the exalted dead of the Confederacy?

(Decoration Day, May 30. You now get a bonus question: What do the letters U.D.C. stand for? United Daughters of the Confederacy.)

(5) Which stalwart but ditsy character in the movie version of *Gone with the Wind* reluctantly obeys Scarlett O'Hara in the birthing scene as Sherman prepares to turn Atlanta into an inferno?

(Prissy, played by Butterfly McQueen. Dock two points from your score if you said Aunt Pittypat. Honestly, Aunt Pitty wouldn't have had the gumption to birth a June bug.)

(6) Between what states does the Mason-Dixon Line actually lie and when was it surveyed?

(Pennsylvania, Maryland, and part of West Virginia; begun in 1763 and completed in 1794 if you want to be right on the money.)

(7) What is the official beginning of Mardi Gras, the South's pre-Lenten blowout?

(Shrove Tuesday, 40 days before Easter. For an extra point, what is a muffaletta? a hero, or hoagy sandwich.)

(8) What does "Mardi Gras" mean in French?

(Fat Tuesday. Throw in an extra point if you can

name the street in New Orleans that is the traditional home of jazz: Bourbon Street.)

(9) What is a praline?

(A rich, sticky, patty-shaped confection made
of brown sugar and pecans. If you have den-
tures, you should opt for a piece of Mississippi
mud pie.)

(10) What beloved literary character cried out, "Skin
me, snatch out my eyeballs, t'ar out my years
by de roots, en cut off my legs, but don't fling
me in dat brier-patch"?

(Brer Rabbit. Score an extra point if you can
name his attacker: Brer Fox. Score an extra
point for Brer Rabbit's creator or the title of the
Walt Disney movie version: Joel Chandler
Harris and *Song of the South*.)

(11) Who was Tom Sawyer's companion while he
searched the river cave for Injun Joe?

(Becky Thatcher. If you said Huck Finn, you definitely need a refresher course in Southern Lit.)

(12) Who wrote "I Dream of Jeannie with the Light
Brown Hair" and "Old Black Joe"?

(Stephen Collins Foster. Quibblers may note
Foster's Northern roots, but they can't deny his
Southland heart.)

(13) What child star was discovered while singing
at the Mississippi State Fair?

(Elvis Presley. Add an extra point if you can
correctly spell the maiden name of his wife:
Priscilla Beaulieu.)

BLUFF YOUR WAY IN
THE DEEP SOUTH

Mary Ellen Robinson Snodgrass

CENTENNIAL PRESS

Centennial Press, Box 82087, Lincoln, Nebraska 68501
an imprint of Cliffs Notes, Inc.

(14) What song from the Civil War hit parade served as the nucleus for Elvis Presley's "Love Me Tender"?

("Aura Lee." Subtract three points if you said "Tenting on the Old Campground.")

(15) What words do the initials C.S.A. stand for, as found on Grandpa's longhandles?

(Confederate States of America. No, Matilda, it's not Crusty Southern Armadillo.)

(16) Why is it a "sin to kill a mockingbird"?

(According to Harper Lee's novel *To Kill a Mockingbird,* the bird sings beautiful songs and does no harm.)

(17) What Louisiana official was known as "Kingfish" and was shot by a state highway patrolman?

(Huey Pierce Long, Jr., dynamic demagogue of Louisiana politics in the 20s and 30s. Give yourself an extra point if you know the title of Robert Penn Warren's novel about the resulting scandal of Long's murder: *All the King's Men.*)

(18) In whose musical did William Warfield sing "Old Man River"?

(Jerome Kern's *Show Boat.* If you said Edna Ferber, you were close, so we won't mark you down; she wrote the novel on which the musical was based.)

(19) How many stars are there on the state flag of Texas, the Lone Star state?

(Only a complete ninny would miss this one.)

(20) What adopted son of the South (born in Pennsylvania) blazed a trail through the Cumberland Gap, was captured by Indians twice, and eventually adopted by the Shawnee Indian chief Blackfish?

(Daniel Boone. If you said Jim Bowie, you're a hundred percent red-blooded [or closeted] knee-jerk Texan and will probably fail this geographically sensitive test. If you said Fess Parker, you don't win any points, but you're probably good at Trivial Pursuit.)

Once you've mastered the rudiments of the Southern canon, you'll hold your own in the best of company. With some polish, you might even transcend the honeysuckle and the kudzu-draped boundaries and, the honor-clad Confederate flag in hand, stand among the sons and daughters of the Old South. But if you *really* want to shine, research the following topics:

(1) the FFV (the First Families of Virginia)
(2) the symbolic meaning of two raised front feet on a sculpted horse bearing the likeness of a Confederate hero
(3) the location of the Swanee River
(4) the key ingredient in spoon bread
(5) the name of Robert E. Lee's horse
(6) the name of Huckleberry Finn's pappy
(7) the number of stars in the Confederate flag
(8) the Crimson Tide and the Bulldogs
(9) the annual date of the "Dixie 500"
(10) the inventor of Coca-Cola

(We won't help you here. To earn your stripes, you have

to take the initiative. After all, this is a crucial period during your rise to the heights of bluffdom.)

Geography

One of the first differentiations a Northern bluffer needs to make is between "south" and "South." True, Florida is deeply Southern, but in no way a part of *genuine* Southernness – any more than Binghamton, the Bronx, or Buffalo. A quick glance over Tampa International or a few moments' stroll down Biscayne Boulevard will convince you. These are shameless Yankee *poseurs* (and doing a piss-poor job of their charade, I might add). Expert bluffers grind their teeth, raise eyebrows in alarm, heave a sigh of disgust, or sniff wordlessly when a rank amateur would-be-Southern bluffer lauds Daytona and St. Petersburg or sings the praises of Key West. So, now that you know the Southern boundary, and where the Mason-Dixon Line is, feel free to wallow in the rich in-between. If questions arise about the outer edges, profess to know little about the frontiers of civilization. In true Southern style, cling adamantly to the past. Resort to memories of your childhood in Little Rock, skinny-dipping along the Pee Dee, struttin' at the annual chittlin' festival in Orangeburg, picnicking in Mobile's Bellingrath Gardens, and autumnal visits to your Grandmammy Walton's grave in Athens (Georgia, of course). Feign perplexity about the environs of apostate states.

The Myth of the Deep South

When someone declares that *all* Southerners speak with a saccharine drawl, *all* Southern men wear

Panama suits, and *all* Southern women flutter their lashes, wade boldly into the fray. Trounce the speaker of such heresy with reminders that hillbillies don't drawl in any flavor of sucrose, white trash don't own suits of any fiber, and crackers couldn't flutter any part of their anatomies if Old Harry himself had them by the tail. Remind your adversary that Southerners come in *many* varieties, and that hillbillies, white trash, and crackers are integral threads among the warp and woof of the true South. Refined or not, they *belong*.

To mask any other lapses in conversation, fill in the gaps with memories of your travels among the bastions of the Confederacy. Recall train rides through Memphis, canoe trips on the Tallahatchie, treks up Stone Mountain, guided tours through the Biltmore Estate, dinner at Antoine's, and photography sessions on the azaleaed grounds of Middleton Plantation. When someone mentions an arcane spot on the map as being "typically Southern"– for example, the view from Biloxi, the Hopewell Ferry, or the recreational variety at Sardis Lake, bluff them one up: pish-tosh them to silence with insistence on the monument to the Wright Brothers' flight at Kitty Hawk, the stalwart Hatteras Lighthouse on North Carolina's outer banks, or the Opelousas Yambilee Festival.

Sneer at any mention of Hilton Head, that renegade stronghold of vulgar, nouveau riche Ohioans and New Jerseyites. Crow at their tacky taste in BMWs and Volvos. Disdain their flashy gold chains and pinkie rings. Hoot at their revolting lack of grace and charm. Come back in spades with rhapsodies about resplendent sunset strolls along the pre-Hugo Battery in Charleston, plates piled high with crawfish and red beans and rice at K-Paul's, or nostalgic retellings of your misadventures during college days at Ole Miss. You'll show them right *quick* where your heart and sympathies lie. No one'll ask to see *your* passport.

Variations on a Theme by Robert E. Lee

To get the most mileage out of any conversation about the South, tie even the most remote spot on the map to some aspect of the Civil War. Look pained when you utter "the Lost Cause" so that your audience will feel your kinship with the great struggle for states' rights. Show blatant disrespect for anything associated with the word "Yankee" (or "damnyankee") — be it a Broadway musical, a brickyard, or a clipper ship. Then ask for a sip of sour mash bourbon — sweet 'n neat — to calm your nerves, which have not been the same since that fateful day of your coming-of-age — the day that Granddaddy Talmadge told you the truth about Gettysburg.

Rely on dramatic posture to carry the day. Gently close your lids, rise resolutely to your feet, and place a trembling right hand over your palpitating heart when anyone hums a snatch of "Dixie." Scorn the Ivy League and the Seven Sisters. Refuse to say the name "Sherman" aloud (he was and still is a despised man). Shed a doleful tear at the least mention of Reconstruction. Do it up right. Your audience will be duly impressed.

If disclaimers bring you too close to the brink of disclosure, tug again the strings of narrative into the distant past. Launch into a full hour of tales about how your Great-Great-Aunt Nanny Lee buried the family silver in the oak churn under a row of sweet tater vines. Confide that Cousin Virginia Lee (twice removed) clung to the sides of a spavined plow mule while concealing herself among okra stalks until Union cavalrymen stopped pillaging the henhouse. (Any double name that ends in Lee is safe, so bluff with confidence. You've got both feet on firm red clay.)

History

Display the greatest regard for stories of the South's early days, when Cotton was king and Tobacco was queen. Reject other royalty. Dwell on a run of virtuosity which will forever establish your expertise. Call up family memories of evening walks along the levee, where sternwheelers churned to a halt in order to discharge sacks of rice and indigo and burlap-wrapped bales of cotton. Breathe the names of Delta plantations, especially Belle Reve and Long Vue, as though you were invoking spirits of a glorious and beloved past.

Fill in chinks of bull sessions with stories about springtime fishing in the Big Ditch (the Mississippi) and fall hunting – shooting your limit of bobwhite quail, snipe, and woodcock. Or talk about uptown matters. Yearn for the days when women were women – in swaying hoopskirts, bobbing parasols, and the smartest of feather-trimmed bonnets from Paris. Badmouth the ERA. Let 'er roll in high gear. Romance is a safe topic, especially if you've seen a few Hollywood versions of the War Between the States or the TV mini-series *North and South*. Let yourself be carried away by waltzing a few steps in grand style or whistling the melody from "Eatin' Goober Peas." You'll score an extra point or two.

Among "learned" fellow bluffers, cite a few lines of

Thomas Jefferson's essays or letters, such as the opening strains of "The Testament of Freedom": "The god who gave us life gave us liberty at the same time. The hand of force may destroy, but cannot disjoin us . . ." When you run dry on that one, cite his comments about the tree of liberty being watered periodically by the blood of patriots and tyrants. Point out self-righteously that the majority of our founding mothers and fathers, including a sizeable number of presidents, had direct ties with Virginia plantations. Then pause for rebuttal. Don't worry—you won't have to duck.

Literature

You don't need a degree from Duke, Rice, or Loyola to appear moderately learned on the subject of Southern literature. Always safe are comments on O. Henry's enigmatic twists or Edgar Allan Poe's phantasmagoric settings and anorexic women. Keep a crib sheet of lines from "A Municipal Report" or "A Retrieved Reformation, " and "The Raven" or "Annabel Lee" for a quick refresher if you wander into an artsy crowd. A safe quibble is whether Thomas Holley Chivers really *did* write the prototypes. Smile and lift your hands as though you know more than you're saying. It's a safe out.

If the exchange runs to heavier artillery, you can rely on the merest mention of William Gilmore Simms's *Yemassee* or any revelation about William Faulkner, such as the name of his fictitious Mississippi county (Yoknapatawpha), the source of the bad smell in "A Rose for Emily," (her late lover), or the patriarch of the Snopes clan (Ab). Ponder aloud in fragmentary stream-of-thoughts about the influence of Faulkner's circular narrative on a myriad of poor imitators.

If hordes of literati come hot on your trail, waffle off in a new direction. Try a rhetorical question about the effect of Hollywood movie scriptwriting on Faulkner's middle years. (A little familiarity is worth *some* mileage.) Quote the part of Faulkner's Nobel Prize acceptance speech that deals with "love and honor and pity and pride and compassion and sacrifice," and the part where Faulkner says, "I believe that man will not merely endure: he will prevail." Who knows—a little prior preparation may win you the whole shooting match.

Bluffing your way through Flannery O'Connor, Eudora Welty, Lillian Smith, Shirley Ann Grau, or Katherine Anne Porter is tricky going. Be sure you know your stuff or you'll find yourself hip-deep in a literary Okefenokee. Gingerly refer to the deep biblical significance of O'Connor's peacocks or to Eudora Welty's rollicking humor in "Why I Live at the P.O." Ask anyone to top "Stella Rondo" or "Wallstreet Panic Snopes" as the best character names in all of literature.

If you feel up to it, broach an analysis of the family hierarchy in *The Condor Passes* or sally forth into the intricacies of stream of consciousness in "The Jilting of Granny Weatherall," or the symbolism in *Old Mortality.* If pressed for details, fall back on veiled comments about the breadth of opportunities for female authors in the South. Assault your detractors with a veritable barrage of examples: Lillian Hellman, Zora Neal Hurston, Caroline Gordon, Ellen Glasgow, Taylor Caldwell, and don't forget Margaret Mitchell and Carson McCullers. Challenge anyone to name a more heartwarming character in Southern literature than

Mammy or Berenice Sadie Brown; they won't stand a chance. If you're fond of *I Know Why the Caged Bird Sings,* write Maya Angelou for permission to use her distinctive call to dinner: "Le grub est servi!" (Aren't you sorry you didn't start bluffing Southern sooner?)

If there's time, delve into the uplifting humor of Florence King, Molly Ivins, or Clyde Edgerton. Quote chapter and verse wherever you find a receptive audience, particularly if the surrounding voices wax thin in the swell of your superior knowledge. Chuckle over fondly remembered lines from *Southern Ladies and Gentlemen* and *Confessions of a Failed Southern Lady* or recent one-liners from *Southern Magazine.* Remember, bluffing is a game of opportunities. It's not how much you know, but how you use each tidbit that counts.

Traditions

Ah, Southern traditions! Here the bluffer par excellence can rise to dizzying heights of rapture, soaring on wings of sheer romantic invention. The range of subjects which Southerners hold dear extends from ghost legends to pirate treasure, holiday cheer to coming-of-age rituals, tales of unrequited romance to family scandals. The good bluffer need only crack a good bottle before breaking into a spiel of yarn-spinning that will lock his lessers in thrall. (Take a deep swig of Southern Comfort, Old Crow, or Jack Daniel's. Real Southerners never hold tippling against you if the label sounds local.)

Booger Tales and Old Legends

Begin with stories of ghosts and "haints" that wind

up in a rattling, belly-wrenching conclusion – such as "The Bride of Pisgah," the tale of the hapless groom who builds his bride a new cabin atop a flawed ledge of rock deep in the Pisgah hills of North Carolina. During the inevitable wedding night, the fire flickers low, luring scores of poisonous snakes out of a cleft in the stone floor toward its waning heat.

The lovers are found horribly disfigured and mis-shapen from multiple fang wounds, their decaying limbs bulging and black with venom. To grace your telling with the right panache, lower your voice as you near the end of the tale. Dwell on the sound of the lovers' plaintive calls as their wraiths seek to reunite in the lonely, tangled wilderness deep in the Appalachian Mountains.

Before the evening palls, launch into an upbeat saga of pirate troves along the isles of the Gulf of Mexico, where José Gaspar and his desperadoes herded virginal blossoms of Southern womanhood. These girls, boarding in Charleston and sailing toward fiances who awaited them in Natchez and New Orleans, met their doom as hostages to sate Gaspar's insatiable lust – for doubloons. By the time the gold exchanged hands, Gaspar, true to his word, passed along the sullied belles to disappointed fathers and ex-future husbands.

The hapless victims, reduced to the level of shop-worn merchandise, languished as old maids, never to know the promised raptures of matrimony, much less the crowning glory of motherhood. (Lay on the adjectives. Southerners have no yen for well-trimmed prose. They prefer marble columns and gingerbread on their architecture and furbelows and curlicues galore on their literature, the gaudier the better. A Southern audience is a bluffer's delight!)

Holidays

If you've got really attentive listeners, interject some Southern cheer. Tell stories about holiday joy, such as the Twelfth Night tradition that sailed from English ports and lodged along the Carolina and Georgia coasts among islanders who flourished apart from the mainland and lost touch with the rest of American society. Regale your audience with minute touches, such as "Little Christmas" songs and games.

Without pause, pass on to the Louisiana "King Cake" tradition, in which one guest finds a gold coin in the Easter cake and reigns as king or queen of the evening's festivities. At this point in your bluffery, play the consummate entertainer. Smile a lot as you lapse into occasional pauses. Go for effect. Hum a few bars of "Oh! Susanna" or "Beautiful Dreamer." They'll love you!

Blood, Guts, Gore, and Violence

On no condition should you favor the womenfolk exclusively. Turn to the males of your audience and ramble on about coming-of-age initiation-into-manhood rites among Southern hunters. Bone up on East Texas pre-Thanksgiving quail and pheasant orgies, Mississippi snipe shoots, and Alabama coon hunts. Reiterate familiar stories about the spilling of hot blood and how first-time hunters have their foreheads swabbed with fresh blood and their shirts cut to ribbons by time-tested hunters.

Swallow your Midwestern distaste for gore. Southern audiences relish violence in all forms, the grosser the better. (If you don't believe this claim, just read a week's worth of headlines from the Charlotte *Observer* or the Atlanta *Constitution*. That'll make a believer out of you.) Wink knowingly at the youngest members of your audience. Make the most of the moment. This opportunity is bluffing heaven.

Hearts and Flowers and Lawsuits

Round out your narration with a lagniappe for the bluehaired darlings in the audience. Throw in a few vignettes of unrequited love or disappointed heirs. Embellish with extremes – the iron-willed matriarch and the disapproving, silver-haired aristocrat, the cringing ingenue and the fawning swain. Punch up stories of the reading of the will with swooning ne'er-do-wells who learn too late that Grandpa Maginnis meant what he said about not marrying that trashy gal from up Missouri way.

Scandalize your audience with stories of the twenty-year-old floozie who won the whole pot after her December groom passed to his reward, leaving her, his second wife, the 25,000-acre plantation. Launch into tirades of how scrabbling, clawing relatives filed suit and tied up the Tidball Railroad fortune in litigation for years to come. Juice up the details with mention of frequent trysts in Baton Rouge, perfume-soaked hankies on the crushed velvet divan, and clandestine rendezvous down logging roads, where hearts beat as one, still-made whisky befuddles the brain, and stolen kisses seal the deal.

If your stock of cliches runs low, check out a few videotapes of *Hurry, Sundown, Raintree County, In the Heat of the Night, Band of Angels,* or *Tobacco Road* for maximum command of details to sweeten the pot. Southern audiences discount cliches so long as they're accurate cliches. A few repetitions or flaws in the logic of the plot don't matter. The main thing is *effect*. Go for it.

Class Structure

As you craft your string of stories, don't forget to keep your social classes straight. America may be the democratic melting pot of the world, but the South remains the classic holdout. Southern aristocrats will forever send their sons to military academies and their daughters to finishing schools. No sweet young thing worth her Tennessee walking shoes will ever step foot into society without a proper bringing out among the elite—complete with a rented hall, thirty-piece orchestra, white-gloved escorts, a six-thousand-dollar designer dress, and all the trimmings. Remember the aristocrat's dictum: the more it costs, the better it has to be.

Learn to distinguish what's merely rich from authentic, Old South luxury. The fireplace is the focus of Southern homes, and it's inevitably graced with an oil portrait, larger than life, of Mama in her misty white debutante gown, shoulders chastely covered by a pouf of voile, her eyelet-and tulle-edged parasol leaning demurely against the davenport. If you find yourself facing one of these atrocities, raise your lead crystal sherry glass in appropriate homage to Southern virginity. Comment on the portrait's display of milk-white skin, long silken lashes, and tiny feet—three virtues that the most awkward and ill-equipped of daddy's girls would die for.

To ingratiate yourself among the cream of society, nod appreciatively at the first mention of connections with the "creme de la creme." When the hostess drops the name of Grandfather Pierre T. Beauregard, who was kin on his mother's side to the Byrds of eastern Virginia and the Sumters of South Carolina, touch her forearm with genuine reverence. Mutter a few comments about your own ties with the James River branch of the Lee family, but, to spare yourself embarrassment, deny any knowledge of a family tree connecting you directly to Light Horse Harry himself. To escape any contretemps, divert attention with your strong knowledge of the Tutherows of Orangeburg or the Tollivers of Savannah.

Among second-degree Southern nobility (and their name is legion), listen attentively for clues to family pride, such as a silver ewer that once graced the baptismal font of the Montgomery Second Presbyterian Church transept. Southerners respect silver above diamonds, platinum, or gold. Southern housewives are said to drop the ironing and abandon feather dusters in favor of polishing enough hollowware to get them through an unannounced visit from Second Cousin Coretta and her kinfolk from Columbia.

Show furrowed contempt for carpetbaggers and interlopers (not unlike yourself) who storm the gates of their betters in order to get a toehold in Southern society. Never, NEVER, force your way into an invitation. Don't even *hint* that you would commit serious infractions of federal law just to hover on the outskirts. Smile expectantly as though the idea of a Sunday afternoon musicale at the Misses Culpepper's comes as a most pleasant surprise. Remain on the edge of the festivities until Miss Aurelia Meade Culpepper herself leads you by the hand into the limelight. Then shine. You've earned the right.

GENERAL SOUTHERN TRAITS

If you're bound and determined to glow among Southerners, you must carefully delineate between who was *really* born in Baton Rouge and who among the crush is feigning. Then your task is easy. Emulate the real belles and beaux and disdain the phonies. Be on the lookout for smiles, accents, language, good manners, a sense of humor, dress, and pedigree. These are the real signs of Deep South gentility.

Distinguishing Marks

Real Southerners tend to smile a lot, producing a disarming, but not unpleasant smearing of vowel sounds. (More about Southern sound in a bit.) They also incline toward kindness and generosity, often pressing gifts of hot pepper conserves and root cuttings of rare aucuba or photinia into the hands of friends and loved ones. They'll share their family secret for the best way of docking a dog's tail or making dry vinegar and pepper barbecue sauce. Accept this sharing with joy and vow to complete the exchange by mailing off that very day your grandmother's recipe for calf's foot jelly (or the pattern for her wedding ring quilt) or your grandfather's secret for wet, smoky barbecue sauce (or the cleanest way to decapitate Carolina sea turtles).

Coarseness, lack of concern for others, and rapid speech are the mark of a Yankee. Watch your behavior and soft-pedal any crasser tendencies, such as an affected "Hee-Haw" laugh, a narcissistic monologue, or the urge to roar through a sentence like a sausage mill in reverse. Remember, Southerners take their time — especially when they have the floor. Do thou likewise.

To detect the genuine Southern woman, look for heirloom jewelry — such as slender chainlink bracelets, delicate strings of coral or lapis lazuli beads, filigree breast pins, or an upswept cascade of curls held in place by graceful, understated matched clasps. Genuine Southern men prefer sedate tie pins or tie bars (You know, those tortuous little horizontal gilhooleys stretching from collar tab to collar tab that force a double Windsor into the Adam's apple.) If you want to cultivate Southernness, take heed and dress accordingly.

Rely on light, wispy fabrics if you are a bluffer of the distaff persuasion. Tie a simple grosgrain or taffeta bow at your waist (if you still have a waist). Brush your hair into a graceful pageboy or chignon. Adorn with a gardenia or fragrant sprig of sweet bubby. Downplay jewelry. A single strand of pearls and a tasteful bangle are sufficient. Leave the gold chains, shoulder pads, and punk coifs to less-well-brought-up Yankees. They never miss an opportunity for overkill.

If you are a male bluffer, go for collegiate suaveness if you still have a semi-athletic physique. Try brown Italian loafers, a navy blazer (with appropriate Latin mottoes on the buttons, of course, like *Lux Libertas* or *In Flagrante Delicto*), and a maize pastel shirt. If you're a golfer or sports fan, bright slacks will rev up your attire. If the social occasion is informal, go for Pepto-Bismol pink or Arnie green or even yellow and olive madras plaid. If the evening is more formal, pale blue summer seersucker with a straw boater and well-polished wingtips is always in style. Avoid rep ties, five-pound belt buckles, and tiger-eye pinkie rings—they reek of Northern gaucheness.

Behavior

As for mannerisms, female Southerners cultivate a light, tinkling laugh and a mild, flirtatious manner heightened by the merest upturn of a coquette's smile. Seat yourself slightly forward in your chair with ankles crossed and slender hands graciously at rest in your lap. (It goes without saying that polite Southern ladies eschew both garish blood-red polish and dagger-length nails.) Incline slightly as if to catch every word from your interlocutor's lips. Lean your head to the side if you want to indicate enjoyment or bemusement. Hide your mouth behind your hand if you venture a laugh.

Male mannerisms are less overt. If you smoke a pipe, clutch it in one hand as you lean back against the mantle or banquette. Or cradle your drink in both hands as you devote strict eye contact to any lady who is speaking. Rise ever so gently from your seat when a woman leaves or enters the room. This motion indicates that good breeding runs in your veins; even if you're suffering a mini-coronary, you still pay your respects to Southern womanhood.

Gently touch your female companions with a hand to the waist or a protective arm about the shoulders, particularly if you're walking over rough terrain in the lower tearose garden or along cobbled streets. Assist women with their wraps. Offer to adjust the air conditioning to suit delicate female constitutions. Even though the average Southern woman learned at an early age to jump stallions, fire grapeshot at trespassers in the watermelon patch, and outdistance hot-blooded male cousins on foot and by water, keep up the traditional pretense that Dixie girls must be sheltered.

Well-bred Southern men would never knowingly offend the fairer sex. Never light up without asking first. Bow slightly when asking for a dance. Smile as though your partner graces your very existence by her willingness. Escort her back to her chair and brush your lips against the back of her hand. You won't believe how much blatant Old World courtliness is worth!

In general, ingratiate yourself with the most polished manners you can muster, particularly at a bar, banquet, or dinner table. Ladies, particularly, should smooth the cutwork linen napkin as though it were the most treasured item in the family store. Gaze rapturously at the twelve-branch candelabra twined with vinca vines and highlighted with ranunculus blooms. Comment on the flower-decked epergne, especially if the blossoms came from Sister Annabelle's peony bed, the Episcopal parsonage's rare japonica collection, or Grandmother Lucretia's prize sasanqua bush. Beam as you compliment the table arrangement and calligraphied menu cards.

Speech, or The Foot in Your Mouth May Be Your Own

Refrain from loud, sudden, or obnoxious epithets (the mark of a no-count Northern varmint or hussy). If you must render emotional commentary, utter a prim "Dear

Gussy," "Law me," "Horsefeathers," "Bless Pat," or "Have mercy!" In less demonstrative situations, a simple "I swan" or "My, my" will do. (For men who fear they would choke on the above suggestions, a shocked "I do declare" is sufficient.)

Note: among less noble Southerners, it's quite proper to up your level of epithets to "I could chew nails and spit tacks," "I don't care a pea turkey damn," and "Shit fire and save matches." For vivid displays of elation, use the ever-appropriate "Hot damn." Exercise caution, however. Even middle-degree Southern womanhood has to be screened from gross crudity.

If, however, you find yourself in a redneck gathering – such as a stockcar race, a fishing party on the Santee-Cooper, or on an all-night pig-pickin – go whole hog. Nobody will get their nose out of joint. In fact, friendly competition among well-juiced epithet-hurlers may curl your toes. It's been known to happen.

Dialects

Dialects are difficult to fake, even for some of the A-1 offspring of the Confederacy. First, you must know the major dividing lines and decide where you belong. To the north of the South – in Virginia and eastern North Carolina – lie the tidewater speakers, inheritors of England's *oo* for *ou* sounds. For example, "There's a moose in the hoose, get him oot!" This dialect takes unexpected sideturns. Don't even think of faking it.

To the west, along the Appalachian divide in Tennessee and western North and South Carolina, resounds the quaint Minnie Pearl and Tennessee Ernie Ford twang of southern mountaineers, commonly called hillbillies. These folk tromp flat-footed on all *r* sounds, final and otherwise. If you have any questions, review the movie version of James Dickey's *Deliverance* or browse through a collection of Al Capp's *Li'l Abner* cartoon strips.

In South Carolina's coastal region lurk small pockets of a dying breed—the speakers of Gullah, the remnant of a Gold Coast slave dialect that only a native-born, low country Carolinian can imitate. Better leave well enough alone and stick to standard English. Even more difficult to duplicate are the Creole and Cajun patois of Louisiana. These too require early childhood learning.

For the easiest dodge, concentrate on the wholesale Southern catchall called "Uncle Remus," the deep Southern drawl regularly mangled on television and in the movies. Media Big Daddies and affected Blanche DuBois-types have for generations overdone the subtleties of the Southern drawl. The rudiments are simple: drop all final *r*'s and soften endings in general.

Take your time. The slower the better. For example, "I'm verra pleased to make your acquaintance," "How do," and "Bye, ya'll." Anything more smacks of rampant Hollywood. Leave the Nashville twang to the pros and stick to a syrupy, "Morning. How'r y'all?" Grin a lot and look down at your feet. People will take you for a distant relative who's either been sick a lot or fallen on hard times. Sympathy will work wonders for your standing.

Sense of Humor, or Smile When You Call Me That, Son!

There's no keener mark of the dyed-in-the-wool

Southerner than an urge to have a good time. Dixie's dearest love a jest. The more genteel crowd will go for refined joshing about food and drink or the weather. A safe remark lies along the lines of "Law, look at that dark cloud. It's darker than Mama's frown after Papa's third George Dickel and branch water." For upbeat compliments, try "Eula Mae, I declare, honey, these angel biscuits are so light that I've worn myself to a flat nub just holding them down on this bread plate."

Among working class Dixieites, fall back on standard *mots justes*. The mill crowd loves oldies-but-goodies. Keep a handy list, such as "tight as Dick's hatband," "hotter'n the hinges of hell," "twitchy as a fart in a hot skillet," or "poor as Job's turkey." Don't forget "old as Methuselah's cat," "nervous as a longtailed cat in a roomful of rocking chairs," "He don't know shit from good apple butter," and "sweating like a whore in church." These oldtimers may have gray whiskers, but the in-crowd still roars at every repetition. Let 'er rip!

Story-Telling

For maximum bluffery, practice a long-winded tale and sprinkle it well with every Southernism at your disposal. Stretch it out so that the telling is half the fun. In the South, longwindedness is a natural talent. Look your audience archly in the eye and make appropriate hand gestures. Favorite topics for the obligatory after-dinner stretcher include dog stories, mule stories, and election stories. If you need to reload your stock, read Eliot Wigginton's *Foxfire*, volumes 1-9.

Be cautious with election stories. Only a first-rate bluffer can weather a knock-down, drag-out battle royal between Southern liberals and diehard Dixie conservatives. If you don't feel up to it, lay low when the fur starts flying. The intricacies of Southern politics may not be your game.

If you want to score bigtime with Southerners, maintain a store of favorite anecdotes about favorite sons – particularly, George Wallace, Strom Thurmond, or Claude Pepper. To avoid ruffled feathers, glide gracefully into a friendly exchange. For example, "Ransom, I d'clare, that Jesse Helms up your way in North Ca'lina is one hell-raising scalliwag. What you got good to say for him?" Then keep smiling as volunteers regale you with sputtering defenses.

When the time is ripe, commence your own yarn. Don't fret if you have to fudge the line between fact and fiction. Whether the topic is Elizabeth Ray, the good ship *Monkey Business*, or Rita Jenrette, embellishment can only enhance the tale. Southerners will love you for your inventiveness.

Stories about religion garner a more generous share of enjoyment, especially if they play one familiar sect against the other or keep to obvious scoundrels and snake oil salesmen like Jim and Tammy Faye Bakker or Jimmy Swaggart. The best stories begin like this: "There was this one-legged hardshell Baptist preacher who got stranded one night in a backwoods Mennonite community . . ."

Keep the telling light-handed and jovial. Stress incongruities. Save scurrilous or vindictive punchlines for war stories. Southerners take their religion as seriously as they do their liquor and hunting hounds. But everybody appreciates a good joke, particularly at the expense of somebody else's beliefs. Laughing at a New Jerseyite's pink Lincoln won't ever be construed as bad manners. It's merely social commentary.

For the height of bluffery, wear the mask of the insider. Relax in a gathering of Virginia gentlemen or Georgia peaches until you have a feel for the flow. Listen for the cadence of their speech and the thrust of their humor. Then throw out a single line or two to indicate that you're no slouch. Don't forget your manners. Grin an appreciative, "Pearlette darlin', you're a flat-footed caution" or "Sometimes I don't know who's funnier, Lester – Moms Mabley, Redd Foxx, or *you*."

Insults

If the situation calls for it, don't hesitate to fling vicious insults. Southerners are masters of spite and disdain. For the insufferable blackguard or cowering daffydill, they may resort to ridicule – for example, "Snakes don't crawl no lower" or "A class-A bedwetter if ever I saw one." For men said to be "soft-spoken": "That sumbitch drinks mai-tais. I ask you, what manner of man likes furrin drinks with little bitty parasols in the top?" For the woman of questionable morals: "Folks around these parts don't cotton to round-heeled trash – if you know what I mean." For a child: "I swear, that young'un don't have walking around goat sense." For Yankees in general: "That fool don't know diddly-squat what he's talking about."

Pedigree, the Lifeline of All Southern Relationships

In any social setting – humorous or otherwise – don't dare overlook pedigree. For some of the greatest opportunities in chicanery and deception, defer to the established aristocrats, particularly those with Old South names like Sumter, Oglethorpe, Ravenel, and some of the ones mentioned in earlier sections. (At this point, you might want to review. In bluffery, attention to detail separates the sheep from the goats.)

With middle-level Southern nobility, emphasize governmental ties, such as the Hattiesburg cousin who served two terms in the Mississippi legislature or the sister-in-law from Valdosta who holds a position on the alumni board of directors for Georgia Tech, or Tom ("Squeezer") Transome, who is on the county's Save-the-Seagulls Rescue Team. These people have earned their place among the chosen. Give them their due.

For your own niche, speak offhand and without boast of small accomplishments on the steering committee of the Charlottesville Society for the Preservation of the Tombs and Monuments of Our Honored Dead. Let it be known that you come from a long line of Confederate colonels. Mention a few examples, like your cousin who holds the district record for consecutive terms as honorary colonel in the Alabama state militia and your brother-in-law, Cloyd Devon, the Macon County deputy sheriff. Make up any number of ties with officialdom. The more you can fake, the greater your prestige among title-hungry climbers.

Animal Bluebloods

Extend your lineage bluffing even to your dogs and horses. Comment to anyone who seems interested that the Dalton bluetick can't hold a candle to the Cape Fear champion line of hunting beagle. Should you encounter opposition (and there are those devotees who will not yield one iota on this polarizing issue), demand particulars. Ask to know the trainer, record of treeings and flushings, conditions under which the dogs are bred, kept, and hunted – even the gauge and weight of shotgun that the hunter prefers. Give your opponent a good going-over.

Profess shock and concern over any detail that strikes your fancy, such as the disconcerting news that the owner feeds his dogs scrambled duck eggs and lightbread. Stand firm on the issue of light- vs. cornbread. Cite problems in whelping from bitches who have been allowed to gorge on biscuits, piecrust, and buttermilk. Dwell on multiple examples of mange, distemper, fits, and whipworms in dogs left to founder on spoonbread and dumplings.

Let the fire flash from your eyes if words fail you. Bluff to perfection with moral outrage in your voice and indignation in your posture. If you can manage it, press a trembling hand over your eyes as you clear your throat. This is an occasion for theatrics. Do it up royal.

HOSPITALITY, OR MARY ELLEN'S HANDY GUIDE TO SOCIAL INTERCOURSE SOUTH OF THE MASON-DIXON

Probably the cheeriest of all greetings to a Southerner's ears is the familiar "Y'all come." It's not an idle invitation. Drop-ins are daily fare. Any knocker at the screen door, however humble or ill-timed, is told to "set a spell" out of good manners and camaraderie. Plates of sugar cookies and fruitcake bars follow generous glasses of lemonade and iced tea. Southerners expect visiting back and forth among friends, neighbors, and especially relatives (a term that extends far beyond Northerners' ideas of who's kin and who's only mildly related). Southerners treat guests right so that when they themselves need a free feed or a cheap bed for the night, they'll know where to find one.

Good Food and Family Reunions (They Belong in the Same Category)

Family reunions are annual or even semi-annual events among many clans. The Robinsons never miss a Labor Day for their annual summer spread (not to be confused with their Christmas breakfast bash.) The Tingles send out runners to neighboring counties to be sure not to miss a single soul. The Tevepaughs have been known to hire a hall and a cadre of caterers to accommodate member Tevepaughs. The Settlemyres start cooking three weeks in advance. At the yearly Thiboudeaux feast, trestle tables invite snatchers and grabbers to load up on filé gumbo, golden pennies, pigs-in-a-biscuit, heavenly hash, étouffée, jambalaya, and plain, unadorned fried chicken legs.

To establish yourself as an insider, work your way into the milling crowd and greet people of all sizes and shapes. Comment on Great-Uncle Roscoe's new pickup with the twin chrome tailpipes and spoked mag wheels. Crow over Miz Stapleton's gingham wrap-around apron and Granny Cater's Avon brooch. Watch out for the dippers and chewers – spit cans are a regular hazard. Lift up the youngest member of the bunch and praise her latest bicuspids. Don't involve yourself *too* early in food. (That's a dead giveaway of the crass Yankee buttinsky.) After all, you came to visit, not stuff yourself.

After you've had a chance to hear all about how the MacNusons' oldest girl run off with some jakeleg working Brahmas at the county fair, express your opinion on a topic of general concern – such as the government's giveaway of the Panama Canal, men walking on the moon (where they obviously have no business walking), or the extent of armyworm damage to the soybean crop. If ever you can't muster a proper comeback, look awed and say, "Is that a fact!" or "What *next?*"

Always bow your head respectfully for grace. Don't expect to catch all the words, but jump at the most important – Amen. Get two plates, since one never seems big enough, and it's chancy to hold out for seconds. Join in the double line at the end of the table and trade witticisms with the folks facing your line. Get loose—it won't hurt a bit.

If someone near you claims to have made the horse-radish cole slaw or the sweet potato pudd'n, out of politeness take a double spoonful between your okra-corn-tomato relish and deviled eggs. Layer on a couple of popovers and scoot a few refrigerator dills in among the paper-thin slices of Smithfield ham, three-bean salad, and roasting ears. Nibble at a stalk of stuffed celery or a watermelon rind pickle as though you can't wait another minute for sustenance.

Taste a few things that may look strange, like hush-puppies, squash casserole, souse meat, soft-shell crab, corncakes, or fried green tomatoes. Let those pot liquors sluice around together on your plate as you pour a big glass of sweetened tea (iced, of course), squeeze on a generous wedge of lemon, and grace the top with a sprig of peppermint. Then locate a seat where the conversation is as lively as the slurping is juicy. You don't need permission to sit down. At family reunions, *everybody's* welcome.

Don't mind a relaxation of Emily Post manners at gatherings like these. Where there's *no* tablecloth and *no* silverware to speak of, it's catch as catch can with paper plates, wooden forks, and no knife at all. Expect to use at least three napkins, especially if chicken and dumplings is your forte. A real bluffer can juggle brimming plates, iced tea glass and utensils, and still manage to wave and grin at Uncle Mel clear across the room.

When it's time to ladle on the desserts, choose carefully and smile into the face that looks eagerest for you to try the Bible verse cake. Chances are, the smiler is the baker. Demand a copy of the recipe for your files. Accept no demurs. Bank your slice with dollops of banana pudd'n and lemon icebox surprise. If you find space, take a piece of chess pie and spoon on a glob of homemade peach ice cream. You won't regret it.

Post-Food Gab

At the end of your feast, lean back, pet the family cocker spaniel, and pick your teeth with the remains of your wooden fork as you ease into the debate as to whether Tuscaloosa's defensive line will hold out this year. Express your disapproval of changes in the Methodist hymnal. Laugh at jokes about Ruby Kay's motorbike, Uncle Royce's toupee, or L. C.'s latest traffic ticket for driving without a windshield. Bluffing like this comes easy. These are home folks.

Among the Elite

If chance brings you out of the hoi polloi into higher-level social events, such as a debutante luncheon, Annie Laurie's bassoon recital, or the iris growers' society benefit and reception, spruce up your act. Wear your best. Smile a lot. Those pearly choppers will earn you a place among the blessed. Compliment without fail.

Don't forget to ask questions, such as the secret ingredient in the bourbon balls or the name of the cook who whipped up that *divine* red velvet cake. (If it was Alma Dean, give her a hug and a pat on her well-padded fanny. If it was Estelle, don't say much. She flat-out stole that recipe from Alma Dean's recipe box.) Assure Norval that despite the fact that his boy accompanied

Annie Laurie, the kid is "all boy." Reject key lime punch in favor of straight Kentucky bourbon, the mark of a real Mississippi mudpuppy. Joke about the fed'ral guvmint.

Overnight Visits

Should you rate an invitation for the night, don't hesitate. Southerners have been known to stay over the Fourth and not get home before Thanksgiving. Some oldtimers take in overnight guests and keep them through three generations. It's mutually satisfying in the South: the inviter loves company as much as the invitee loves hospitality. Like yin and yang, the two feed off each other's egos. A perspicacious bluffer will relax in these surroundings and shine like new money.

When possible, offer to help. Take time to sit on a cane-bottomed side-porch rocker and read the evening *Times-Picayune* with the head of the household. Gaze out at the rich, new-plowed acreage and comment on how much the sorghum and field peas have grown since the spring rains. Accompany your host on an evening's stroll down rows of Seneca chief to assess this year's smut damage or to test-milk a few kernels of bantam silver queen. A better-than-average bluffer can weather any agricultural bluffery with a few snorts about new-fangled farming methods and a wave of dismissal in the general direction of those university-trained, but callow Department of Agriculture boys.

Southern housewives are notoriously fussy about getting the chores done. Should the lady of the house look overburdened, offer to make beds, but *only* if you can stretch the counterpane tight enough to bounce a quarter to the ceiling. It you aren't that up on housewifery, insist on sitting on the stoop and shelling butter peas, stringing beans, or cutting corn off the cob to help out with the summer canning. Even offer to wash fruit jars and sterilize zinc lids and rubber rings. An expert bluffer can fake Southern charm by joining the young'uns for a lightnin' bug hunt, chinaberry barrage, or twilight game of fox 'n hounds. Your amusement of wiggly children will be most welcome.

Gratitude, Gratitude

When the opportunity comes to move on, take your time. Kiss everybody, even the help and the family St. Bernard. Wave affectionate farewells from the door, front porch steps, end of the slate walkway, gazebo, or gravel drive. Honk your horn as you drive out of sight toward the interstate. Southerners love lavish displays of affection. Don't disappoint them.

Follow up with gushy thank-you notes (You know, the ones with bluebirds and curly initials in the upper lefthand corner.) Tuck in a hostess gift, such as a copy of your grandmother's Caroline County version of cheese grits and whole hog sausage. If your stay was extensive, wire a lidded willow basket of gourmet dewberry jellies or a mixed arrangement of anthurium, baby's breath, ivy sprigs, and a few birds of paradise. Largesse is the mark of the Southern guest.

To decorate your home Southern style, let your bookshelves do homage to Old South recipes. Stock up on *Southern Living* collections. Look for oldie-goldies like *Country Roads: Menus from Our Past, White Trash Cookin', Market to Market,* or *The Junior League's All-*

Star Parade of Dessert Favorites. Grace your kitchen's outlay of modern gemcrackery with tasteful country touches—a branch of dried bittersweet and a handful of money plant in hobnail glass, an occasional antique doughtray, an heirloom pie safe, or a well-used flour mill. For good measure, hang up some herbs in the pantry. It's a homey touch.

Bluff a bit about how your grandmother taught you *never* to stir the oatmeal muffins more than six rounds or how your father added half an eggshell and three pinches of chicory to his coffee to make it shine. Divert suspicion that you are bluffing by asking pertinent questions about other people's red-eye or sawmill gravy. Take notes.

Drink

Keep a well-stocked bar, including Rebel Yell, Wild Turkey, Southern Comfort, and Panther Piss. Offer a choice of Dr. Pepper, Sun Drop, Cheerwine, and diet R.C.'s for the children and footwashing Baptists. Southerners like tall glasses and lots of ice, which cuts down on frequent refills. Lead your sippers out on the verandah or under the weeping willow for a late evening view of the distant Chattahoochee or a congenial counting of martins and barn swallows.

Point out your neighbor's ill-fated efforts to combat honeysuckle and kudzu. Comment on the virulence of mosquitoes and no-see-'ems since the county dammed up Jacob's Fork Creek and let the overflow deluge your lower forty and flood your septic tank. (Thoughtful Southerners light up the citronella; Northerners merely pass around the bug spray.) Don't escort your guests inside for the night until bats fly over and treefrogs begin to call. Sultry nights are good for something besides bug bites and sweat. Sit back and enjoy nature's symphony.

Festive Occasions

For bigger celebrations like Christmas Eve, haul out the chased-silver punch bowl and cut-glass cups. Keep a small silver bell close at hand to summon the hired help. Put white gloves on the maid and butler. Make a big to-do over fresh-ground nutmeg on the eggnog and warming pans for the hot cinnamon yeast rolls. Offer mugs of hot cider with orange peel, clove garnish, and cinnamon stirring sticks. Raise your glass spiritedly to the holiday season. In the South, gesture is all. The bigger the gesture, the better the bluff.

Practice toasts that play up Southern weaknesses— legend, land, and lineage. Wish the best to a newly engaged couple or the sire of the family clan. Note the passage of years. Allow yourself to get choked up and teary-eyed over new additions to the family, the passing of Great-Grandpa Pierce to his eternal reward, or the recent addition of a church bell to the Elmyra Presbyterian Church's rebuilt steeple. Wish that life may go on as it has for generations. You won't be far off the very thoughts of your guests.

Entertainment

Fortunately, you don't have to go to too much trouble for most Southerners; as long as there's someone to talk to, there's no need for formal entertainment. Just keep the snack food coming. Rednecks, who are world-class snackers, love humble fare. Skip the petit fours, aged brie, and creme de menthe and lay on the pigs feet, sausage biscuits, and pink pickled eggs.

Penrose on cocktail picks with a cherry tomato or stuffed olive on top is Buckingham Palace quality eats for working class Southerners. In a pinch, fried liver mush on lightbread will suffice. Rednecks may be socially offensive, but they aren't picky when it comes to food. Expect to hear, "Johnetta, this is *good* groceries!"

Impress blueblooded guests with your Southern elan. Spread the table with a variety of goodies. Deep South banqueters respond to number and variety of dishes over cost and/or quality. Mix your serving pieces for maximum effect. Emphasize antique crockery bowls heaped with crab dip or carnival and milk glass filled with plain old Georgia peanuts and nacho chips.

Intersperse sweetgrass baskets filled with hot snacks. Put jalapeña peppers, fresh chilies, and a full jigger of Texas Pete in the salsa. Toast tiny oysters under the broiler and serve with hot seafood sauce. You won't have to wrestle with leftovers.

Strummin' and Pickin'

Invite anybody with a musical instrument to bring it along. This type of pickup musicale has been flavoring Southern get-togethers since the Hatfields met the McCoys. With no prior arrangement you may find yourself in the midst of a downhome box-pickin', foot-stompin', plug chewin' rendition of "Rockytop" or "Cripple Creek." Juggers and washboard strummers usually wade right in with Jew's harpers and kazooists not far behind. They're not proud.

Nobody needs direction. If you lack experience with country pickin' and singin', sit to one side of the gathering and pat your foot. Clap on the offbeat, nod appreciatively, and act demented. No one will ever know you're bluffing.

Poker and Fresh Gossip

Among small groups, set out the cards and poker chips and step back. Poker is as much a part of Southern menfolks' entertainment as polkas are of Polish weddings. But watch out for the sedate, refined Old South gentlemen – they're the first to take you to the cleaners. If you feel at a loss for words in close company, review choice Southern epithets: "Have mercy," "So help me Hannah," and "Law me." After a couple of Jim Beams and coke, one-liners are the order of the day: "Hell far" and "Shee-it."

For "women only" social occasions, such as wedding and baby showers, secretaries' luncheons, and Tupperware and Fuller Brush parties, follow the same general guidelines. Let the talk flow as long as it will. Interest yourself in general gossip and relish local scandal. Prod for details. When all else fails, make up some. You can be sure they'll be appreciated and passed on.

When the tale of the day is spun out, start a new round of conversation about grandchildren, courting couples, acts of God, acts of adultery, and other items of local interest. Question career women about their rise to stardom in the bookkeeping department at the sawmill or their latest advance to head nurse or head librarian. Get the schoolteacher in the bunch (there's always at least one) to describe the latest "trend" in public education. A real bluffer covers a lack of information with questions, questions, questions.

For mixed gatherings, keep it light. Drift from group to group and enjoy the joviality that colors every Southern social event — from the seventy-first annual volunteer firemen's pork barbecue to the Delta Dek Bridge Club luncheon. Bluff your way with affability and genuine delight in the trivia that comprises small-town activities and big-city concerns — the same things work in Tutwiler or Jackson. (Note: Don't assume that Southern women are the only ones who relish a fresh morsel of gossip. Menfolk have their ways of spreading the news.)

Watch yourself after too many trips to the punch bowl. A loose tongue has tripped many a bluffer. If you come close to discovery as a charlatan amongst red-blooded Confederates, call attention to the fact that you're dressed for success. Display your Day-Glo rebel-flag T-shirt with the portrait of Colonel Sanders on the back. It's a sure-fire showstopper.

SOUTHERN LIFESTYLE

It's a rare bluffer who can't carve him- or herself a comfy niche in the environs of the Deep South. Sure, there are adjustments to be made, especially with certain terminology—like the difference between riff-raff, clodhoppers, and peckerwoods. For those who hail from Madison, Wisconsin, you'll need to relearn the meaning of toboggan—in Mobile, it's not a sled. It's a knitted stocking cap. (For further clarification, turn to the glossary at the end of this guide. Pore over every word and practice every day. It'll be a big help.)

Another difference is the flora and fauna, which often seems threatening to neophyte bluffers who have never thrashed a path through overhanging wisteria tendrils, dickered with an irate alligator, encountered a scorpion with stinger raised at the ready, or faced off against a timber rattler. But these are minor challenges, which well-aged bluffers know in advance how to counter. As Teddy Roosevelt would advise, "Speak softly and carry a big stick."

All things considered, you won't find a more pleasant place to lay your head. One proof of the allure of a Southern address is the rapid movement south of people in the North who are tired of traffic jams, pollution, high fashion, and snow shovels. (True, the South is rapidly becoming polluted with carpetbaggers, but we're doing our best to combat the situation.) The wise bluffer will steer clear of parvenu Dixieites lest somebody put two and two together and decide that you're one too.

Residence

One fact of Southern life that's hard to bluff around is the stateliness of Deep South mansions. Along the levee road out of New Orleans are gracious front porches flanked by Mississippi steamboat gingerbread or fluted Greek revival columns and welcoming lanterns in the hands of iron pickininnies that form the stereotypical image of Southern hospitality. Pleasantly walled in by filmy wisps of Spanish moss among the giant arms of live oaks and cypresses, the wraparound verandahs lend themselves to romantic illusion on a grand scale. Bluffers should rapidly incorporate these illusions.

To immerse oneself in a Southern lifestyle is to kick back and free oneself of compulsions and inhibitions. Nobody in the South is ever in a hurry, as traffic down two-lane Southern backroads will quickly convince you. If you get caught behind a hay wagon, 8-N Ford, or cornpicker (or all three) headed for the barn, don't stew or chafe Yankee style. Blow your horn and wave a friendly greeting. Roll down your window and chew the fat. Southern lifestyle is at its best when it's congenial and low-geared. The consummate bluffer should move at a reduced pace for maximum deception.

When the sultry afternoon heat reaches its zenith and humidity shimmers in the air, true scions of the South will excuse themselves for a leisurely nap (often called a "sinking spell"), which may be taken on the upstairs chaise behind closed shutters, across the foot of a fourposter under a paddle fan, or in the wicker glider on the downstairs porch. Following a suitable rest, the bluffer should yawn, stretch as languidly as a porch gekko, and reach for a glass of lemonade. Then with renewed zest, bluffer and companions may make their way to the library.

Indoor Splendors

As a rule, Southern libraries contain moldy, leather-bound volumes of long-forgotten works, such as the philosophical observations of Beauregard Farquhar, the essays of Azalea Adair, or the poems of Martin Tup-per. During a late afternoon of matching wits with the local literati, prove your worth by slipping in a good word for William Byrd, colonial diarist, and his successor, John Pendleton Kennedy, author of *Swallow Barn* (the definitive depiction of plantation life until *Gone with the Wind*). Quote a verse or two from William Gilmore Simms's *Swamp Fox*

> We follow where the Swamp Fox guides,
>   We leave the swamp and cypress tree,
> Our spurs are at our coursers' sides,
>   And ready for the strife are we.

or comment on ribaldries culled from Augustus Baldwin Longstreet's *Georgia Scenes.*. Refer to Bob and Billy's fight in the Courthouse square: "'At were some *fight.* As I recollect, Bob lost his left ear *entirely.* And a piece of his left cheek. And Billy lost part of his nose. Some fight, *I* tell you."

Ladies who want to evoke a genteel aura should claim to have an affection for Kate Chopin's *The Awakening,* George Washington Cable's *Creole Days* or the doomed passion of Bras Coupé from *The Gran-dissimes*. A thorough coverage of the range of Southern poetry suggests the obvious—Sidney Lanier, Donald Davidson, John Crowe Ransom, or Allen Tate. If possible, learn by heart "Bells for John Whiteside's Daughter," "Lee in the Mountains," or "Ode to the Confederate Dead." And don't you dare omit "Lee" from Steven Vincent Benét's *John Brown's Body*. Comment to your audience that Benét was one Yankee Yalie who *understood* how Southerners feel about our "late unpleasantness."

Heirlooms

For visitors to the finer of the Southland's stately homes, correct bluffery requires attention to antiques—particularly heirlooms. Most Southerners keep a variety of faded sepia-toned photographs or daguerreotypes in silver filigree frames or strategically placed lockets. Fall back on the bluffer's standard ploy: ask your host for details about the figures in the pictures. To extend your bluff, comment, "As I live and breathe, Estelle, that man looks just like my Great-Great-Uncle Mabry, who fell at Antietam while trying to relieve the wounded drummer boy of his burden. So help me Hannah, there's a marked resemblance, es*pecia*lly about the nose and mouth."

The respectful bluffer will clutch the family album to his or her heart and ask in a hesitant voice, "Oh, I hope you don't mind, Miz Garrou. I'm *such* a sentimentalist when it comes to memorabilia. *May* I?" Then thumb through the pages with all the reverence of Galahad handling the Holy Grail or Mammy defending the honor of Miss Ellen's portieres. Touch notable entries with loving and respectful fingers.

Squelch the urge to snicker. Shake your head occasionally and ponder aloud, "How like your Mayhew relations you are, Fanny Lou. Why, your chestnut hair has that same glint. You and this gorgeous figure in the Edwardian batiste could pass for twins!" Sure, bluffing requires some outright stretchers, but 300-pound Fanny Louise Ravenel, who dresses like the Pointer Sisters and walks like a four-gaited mare, will clutch you to the bosom of the Mayhew family for this little white lie.

Pass on to the mantle and marvel at the graceful shape of the crystal teardrops that embellish the sconces on either side of Great-Aunt Isadora Bucknell's portrait. Learn the proper terms for every heirloom — from the lavabo to the harmonium, the bootjack to the stereopticon — and *oo* and *ah* accordingly. Don't forget to praise such genuine niceties as oak tongue-and-groove flooring, mahogany fireboards, foddy-gotz hand-crocheted antimacassars, rose glass inserts, and turn-of-the-century bentwood rockers. You don't find *those* in the subdivisions of New Rochelle.

Flutter about the second best parlor with delight. Pull back embroidered pillows and lace curtains from Antwerp to examine slave-made ironwork grilles, balconies, and fences. Show that you're in the know by differentiating between rococo and baroque detail work. Refuse to accept your hostess's self-effacing modesty. Praise Old South decor to the rafters, even if it gives you nightmares and impedes your digestion.

Listen for the hundredth time to stories of how Sookie and Granny Camellia Rose Peabody lowered the cut-glass chandelier (the one the blockade runners brought straight from Nîmes) into the Lowdermilks' hand-dug well when Yankees breached homeguard defenses and battered Decatur. Cluck your tongue sympathetically as though you could see it all before you – from Pickett's Charge to Sherman's March to the Sea. Twitter words of comfort to great-great-great-grandchildren who still mourn the passing of a more civilized society. End the conversation with an appropriate, "Ah, me, Myrtle Mae. More's the pity. It's a shame and a disgrace how good people must suffer."

Garden Delights

Dry your eyes conspicuously and insist on a complete inspection tour of the grounds to lighten the moribund tone of the afternoon. Catch Sarah Beth's hand and stroll among the feverfew and chrysanthemum beds and down the liriope-lined walkways. Stop to pull a sprig of pink spirea for your hair or lapel. Comment on how fresh the hollyhock bed looks when the sun sets over Tupelo. If the gardening was done by Sarah Beth herself, patronize, patronize. (Liberation of Southern womanhood will take at least three more generations. Don't be surprised at four or five.)

On the brick walk to the boxwood garden, step energetically, but not too fast for Southern strollers. Halt occasionally, sip your limeade and rum, and breathe in the sweet redolence of butterfly bush and privet hedge. If raindrops threaten your outing, stop off at the gazebo at the first sign of moisture.

Perch eagerly on a wrought-iron loveseat and listen to Sarah Beth's lecture about the use of ground pecan shells as a suitable mulch for laurel and dogwood or dousings of hot pepper as a means of halting fire ants. Interject your own remedy for Japanese beetles, which includes running them up in the blender and spraying them onto prize clematis vines. Throw in an offhand remark about those ornery hurricanes that swoop up the coast and spoil everybody's Labor Day fun.

Ask for the details of Aunt Thelma Faustina's latest addition to the Japanese waterfall or Cousin Joe Parks's purchase of a family of pottery rabbits. Pose for photos atop the half-moon bridge. Throw in your own experiences at Brookgreen Gardens, when the Upchurches took you walking among the statuary and you fainted from the heat. Lay it on thick about your passion for topiaries. No one will ever guess that you've never ventured outside Pittsburgh until this moment.

Dress

For recreation at the beach or along the bayou, dress Southern style in cut-offs and chop-tops. On cooler days stick to fresh-pressed and starched chinos and top-siders or puckered cotton shifts and flip-flops. By all means, go barefoot when weather permits, but watch out for sandspurs and mussel shells. Keep your head covered, preferably with a cool straw hat or STP cap. Real Southerners know the strength of the sun and guard their complexions. Don't let a little slip-up like third-degree sunburn blow your cover.

If your hair looks like who-shot-Liz from too much wind and salt water, braid it or tie on a bandanna. Expect a quick change from your natural color to horsetail blonde, with alterations in texture to match. Southerners don't fret much over the ravages of hot weather. In fact, Southerners don't fret much over anything – short of running out of barbecue sauce,

Uncle Earl's two-week toot at Natural Bridge with that Phillips woman, or (heavens forbid) a family inter-marriage with infidel Yankees. So keep it casual. Your bluffing will carry the day.

Sport Clothes

For local football games, you might have to rev up your style. If the teams are local high school or college, preppy regalia is in order. Navy blue strikes most people's fancy, whether in sweaters or sweat pants. Duck into a local pawn shop and scare up some frater-nity or sorority jewelry with which to emblazon your-self. Before you know it, you'll have friends you never knew who remember you from the time you and the Dalton brothers poured strawberry gelatin into Bethena's soaking unmentionables. Or the Thanks-giving holiday that you stocked up on chicken feed and guinea hens, which you conveniently locked into your rival's dorm room until school reopened. Laugh like a pure fool and no one'll suspect you're bluffing.

If the sporting event takes place at a university, preen before your mirror and make yourself as pre-sentable as possible in a tweedy suit, vest, mono-grammed shirt, and silk tie. Splash on a modicum of Bay Rum. This is a strutter's opportunity. Air out your flask and fill it with bourbon, the Southern answer to nectar of the gods. You won't need a bluffing strategy if your opponents are well sauced, so pass the flask. When it comes back your way, pass it again.

Dressy Clothes and Uptown Manners

Should you find yourself among churchgoers, refine your university football-going clothes a bit and douse the flask. This is the Southerner at his or her most austere (and hypocritical). Follow Wilbur Lee's lead. Sit still and bow your head with the others. They'll never guess that you've never been to a Wednesday night prayer meeting in your life, much less that you've never been baptized. If you attend high church services, watch how you bend those knees. Kneeling rails can be treacherous on panty hose. Getting back up is also bad on old war injuries.

When in the company of working-class Southerners, don't overdo the polish. Redneck church worship seldom requires gloves, hat, and veil, or tie and coat, so don't tip your hand by overdressing. Watch the others when the shouting begins. If speaking in tongues or rolling in the aisles is in order, you may have to cultivate a coughing spell and go out for a breath of air and a lozenge. As I've said before, some things just can't be faked.

Teas are another occasion that require meticulous care. Southerners love a chance to shine up the family silver and lay it out for inspection. Don't be fooled into thinking that a fortieth wedding anniversary is the reason for the gathering. It's not. Southerners love conspicuous display, especially when there's company from out of town.

Watch yourself at the tea table. Those homemade mints are killers on the waistline and spell death if incipient diabetes runs in your family. Sip lightly at the mint tea and nibble at the cream cheese ribbon sandwiches and the fruitcake fingers. Have a few cheese straws, a hazelnut or two, and call it a day. Staying too long is the sign of a nosy outsider. Ostensibly, you're a Southerner. Size up the situation and move along.

On your way out the door, pay your respects to the hostess and make her believe that you wouldn't have missed her afternoon "do" for the world.

Education

Southerners of the aristocratic stripe expect college degrees among their scions. "Education" isn't necessary (in fact, too much book learning is regarded as downright communistic), but four years' attendance at a suitable institution *is* obligatory. If you're called upon to prove your membership in the breed, sigh nostalgically over evening bull sessions on the roof of the old Delta Tau house.

Recall the day that you presented your senior recital in Hill Hall or donned cap and gown and walked across the stage at Aycock Auditorium. If pressed for particulars, remark that too much information might give away your age. All Southerners are deceptive on that subject. You won't have to say another word.

Listen attentively to long spiels about Southern children away at school. Show proper interest in how they're progressing in equestrian skills or fraternity hierarchies. Don't bother to question majors or GPAs. Southerners show little regard for pointy-headed math whizzes and computer jocks. They're grateful when their offspring get a degree and return home to run the family plywood business or peanut farm.

Music

Look forward to Southern music of all types, but

straighten out your facts before locking horns with real pros. There's a vast difference between rockabilly and Appalachian folk tunes or bluegrass and Dixieland. A zither is a long way from a steel guitar. "Up a Lazy River" does *not* belong in the same breath with "Counting Flowers on the Wall." The sound of Bill Haley and the Comets bears little resemblance to Nashville radio's *Old Time Gospel Hour.* For the minimum chance of letting the cat out of the bag, brush up on all branches of Southern music.

Listen to the car radio on your drive South. Hum along with gospel gold, such as "Will the Circle Be Unbroken," "When They Ring The Golden Bells," and "I Heard the Wreck on the Highway, But I Didn't Hear Nobody Pray." Sing over all seventeen verses of "Amazing Grace" until you can belt them out in your sleep, particularly if you plan to do late-night drinking with real Southerners. It's their after-hours theme song.

Get the facts straight about the personal lives and fortunes of country singers, particularly the women. Most folks around Tennessee take Dolly Parton seriously and frown on too many crude remarks about a lack of sunshine making for small feet. Clear up any questions you may have about Loretta Lynn and Patsy Cline. It's the former who bakes biscuits and the latter who died in the plane crash. True country music fans would never fail to make the distinction.

Dancing

Practice up on clogging, cotton-eye Joe, buck and wing, and the two-step, especially if you're barhopping in East Texas. Somebody might ask you to dance. If dancing isn't your field of bluffery, feign varicose veins or bursitis in your hip. Should your partner take no excuses, step on his or her toes enough to end the charade before you're in too deep. Get back to home territory as fast as possible. Mourn the passing of Mickey Gilley's and send the waiter for more nachos and Dos X's.

On the east coast, anybody with goat sense and a modicum of sobriety can fake shagging to beach music. A level shuffle and controlled, fluid arm movements will carry you through. Sing along to "Under the Boardwalk." (Don't get confused and whistle "Little Deuce Coupe." That's the other coast.) Bluff your way to the bar for enough beer and salt-and-pepper catfish to keep you busy until the band takes a break. Then start building a castle out of Hamms cans. You'll drum up a crowd in no time. Graciously pass the top layers on to a challenger. Folks will think your mama gave you good upbringing.

At harvest time, expect a hoedown. Do your best to get out of this one, because square-dancing requires a certain amount of skill and practice. Clap a lot and enjoy the music from the sidelines. Don't cringe at the sound of rebel yells. When Southern country folk get liquored up and involved in their music, they have to express their sense of belonging. For maximum bluffery, try a rebel yell of your own. If someone presses you to get off your duff and take part in one of the squares, tell 'em that you grew up Baptist and have no idea how to dance. That should tell 'em where *you* stand.

Light Recreation

Southern people are not known for strenuous out-door activities. Most Southerners over thirty are content with sedentary pleasures – such as sittin', rockin', and fannin' – or spectator sports, like the Greater Marietta Open or the Birmingham Classic. A few hardy souls go in for Olympic riding, jumping, swimming, and diving, but the average, youthful citizen of Dixie chooses activities that don't work up a sweat. If you're smart, you'll side with the latter group.

Horseshoes

A major pleaser revived by President George Bush is pitching horseshoes, which definitely falls into the working class category. Parks and playgrounds usually come equipped with sandboxes or sawdust pits. Horseshoes are usually close by, since only a Yankee loser bothers to steal a rusty, weather-beaten horseshoe. Bluffers will be pleased to learn that horseshoes is the only sport in history which gives points for missing. If you can chunk beer cans at the dumpster, you can bluff your way through this sport.

Croquet

Another Southern biggie is croquet, which suits the wide expanse of Bermuda grass or Kentucky blue that Southerners cultivate and groom like orchids in a hothouse. To play croquet, you need only the barest minimum of skills. The idea of the game is to roll your ball through the hoops and prevent your opponents from getting to the final stake before you do. Now, you can manage that, can't you? I thought so. Bluff with confidence.

Fishing, Freshwater and Salt

If you bluff well and slip into Southern confidence like a greased pig in a chute, you may receive the supreme invite—a day at somebody's private fishing hole. Dedicated fishermen take fishing as seriously as the Pope is religious. They employ all manner of evasive action to keep encroachers out of their private stock. A well-tended fishing spot is carefully baited with loaves of bread and fishmeal cake. Nesting grounds are salted with tree limbs and leftover Christmas trees. A wise bluffer will pay proper respect to these preparations.

Duffer fishing is an even safer bet for bluffers. No son or daughter of the South dares cast a slur on the dockside angler. A Dixie tradition that predates Hoagy Carmichael's "Gone Fishin'," bobbing a cork with a cane pole and drowning a few night crawlers and catalpa worms is as relaxing a sport as you're apt to find this side of championship hammocking. All it requires is quiet, relaxation, minimal paraphernalia, and an occasional glance out of one eye. For bluffers with children, here's the place to make your mark. Just cast out, plunk down, and let down your sails.

Saltwater fishing, on the other hand, is a horse of a different color. Expeditions to the coast usually mask other endeavors, such as the consumption of a few gallons of smooth sipping bourbon, an all-night poker party, or hanky-panky with a willing woman. Whatever the ruse, most Southern fishermen sport a glazed and taxidermied trophy of epic proportions in their den or rumpus room to keep up appearances. This is one aspect of Southern life that female bluffers need not concern themselves with. They won't be invited. Ever.

After-Sport Eating

After a brisk game of horseshoes or croquet or a day of trolling and fly-casting, amble back to the back porch for the crowning outdoor sport of them all – barbecuing. Kibbitz on the cook's preparations by insisting that the grill be rubbed down with peanut oil, or the coals be stoked with mesquite chips and the entree be basted with bottled Jamaica smoke. Supervise the cutting of the lemons and limes. Stick a tentative finger into the barbecue sauce, give it a tentative and thoughtful lick, and suggest more or less hot sauce or a couple of pinches of brown sugar. (There are few Southern recipes that don't call for at least a pinch.)

Bluff along when returning sportsters begin to fill their plates with chopped and sliced pork barbecue, barbecued chicken quarters, barbecue slaw (the spicy red kind), barbecued shrimp kebabs, barbecued rainbow trout, and barbecue bread. Dig in with the crowd. Wash it down with cold beer or iced sun tea. Don't talk too much. This isn't the time to wax eloquent. Just pack it in while it's available. If someone asks your opinion, lay on the charm and praise the cook's expertise. If I know Southern barbecuers, you won't be far wrong.

Serious Recreation

There's always the chance that you may have to bluff your way through more serious sports. One example (which is nigh-on impossible to bluff) is horseback riding. From the cradle to the grave, rural Southerners spend more time in the saddle than behind the wheel. They speak knowledgeably about geldings and gaits, bays and sorrels, tack and sulkies. This is one time that deception must be above good to pass muster.

If you know absolutely nothing about the sport, then say nothing. Chances are that equestrians and equestriennes of the braggart variety will welcome your silence so that they can show off. Let them. Spend some time examining blue ribbons and reading pedigrees. Rub a few horse noses and admire the track. Whatever you do, *don't* climb aboard if you don't know a pommel from a pastern.

If you're urged to saddle up, plead allergies. Intone your words through your nose so that anyone can see that you're suffering from all the horse dander. Another worthy ploy is to hide behind a camera lens and declare to any who seem interested, "I've got a lifelong photo collection of Appaloosas in action. The late afternoon sunlight is about right, so I think I'll get a few shots of that filly in the back paddock. Anyone want to join me?"

Another craze among Southerners, particular the lower classes, is stock-car racing. Again, if you know little about split manifolds and roll bars, say nothing. Admire unrecognizable models as "a damn fine piece of racing machinery." Catch the names of a few notables among racers, such as Richard Petty, Darryl Waltrip, Buddy Baker, or Cale Yarborough. To show that you've been an aficionado since diapers, hark back to Junior Johnson, Ned Jarrett, and Fireball Roberts. Speak the last name with particular reverence, now that he's passed on to last-lap heaven.

To stir up conversation and establish credibility,

interject a note of controversy. Mutter a few contemptuous remarks about Janet Guthrie having the audacity to enter a man's sport. (If you're a liberated woman, lean the other way and decry Guthrie's raw and unsportsmanlike treatment by racing's macho in-crowd.) Then grab your binoculars and follow the action on pit row. With luck, a smash-up will divert attention from you to the far turn.

SOUTHERN PHILOSOPHY, OR HOW TO BEHAVE DURING THE PLAYING OF "DIXIE"

A real Southerner doesn't have to be nudged into a recital of beliefs. The tenets of Southernism come into play almost every day, especially when touchy subjects arise, particularly religion and politics. Debate is mother's milk to Southerners, who grew up in the swirl of controversy and can handle themselves well in any exchange. Tread lightly. A lax bluffer can trip up in this company. Get a firm hold on your credo before you venture into the lists.

Southern Controversies

Southern concerns have never been sanguine. Locals are fierce defenders of the faith and often draw blood when words fail, even if the subject is as harmless as the key ingredient in hoppin' john. At one time, Southern-style racism came in for more than its share of outside interest, but that's mainly the liberal Yankee press at work. They have to write about something, so they jack up the newsworthiness of a bit of violence and have the whole South looking like bigots.

A hundred years ago, membership in the Ku Klux

Klan or the White Camellia may have made local sense, but today nobody with any class bothers with such neolithic hoorahing. Wearing pointed sheets and riding horseback through the night has given way to modern open-mindedness. The concerned bluffer will profess a staunch show of ethics and leave these sensitive topics strictly alone. They deserve to die in peace.

Other issues stir Dixie dandies to a pique – such as who dates their sisters and where the fence post belongs at the end of the pasture. Because of this territorial persnicketiness, interfamilial disputes and land squabbles account for more mayhem in the South than in other parts of the U.S. But not to worry. Most of the time, Southerners are too slow-moving and gracious to take offense. As always, bluff with a smile and a suitable greeting. This guise will carry you through most altercations without fail. (If not, don't hesitate to rev up a good pair of legs.)

Firearms

It's also true that Southerners revere guns above any piece of furniture in the house, even the old upright piano or burlwood grandfather clock. To separate a Southern male from membership in the NRA would take an act of Congress. No right-thinking politico who wants to be re-elected would try it. For the time being, the South remains a bastion of violence. The bluffer must tread with prudence in these areas or else wind up a poor second at a turkey shoot with a bunch of partying redneck roustabouts.

Since hoisting a shotgun for the first time can result in a badly bruised shoulder and tears in the eyes from the impact, the bluffer should boldly declare, "Grand-ma Willett made me swear off firearms ever since my daddy shot the hood ornament off her Reo by mistake. It's a family scandal at our house." Southerners respect internal strife and won't press you further.

Cures

On the other side of the coin, Southerners know a great deal about curing the body as well as how to blow it apart. From camomile tea for upset tummy, to poppy-seed tea for diarrhea, to fennel tea for flatulence, granny women have cured the Southern digestive tract with home remedies since before the Revolution. Faking your way among authentic herbalists is risky. Divert conversation with a few recipes if you dare. Try this line: "I haven't had a cold since I was knee-high to a katydid. Mama always rubbed my chest with sassafras and elderberry salve and kept my cup filled with birchleaf and dandelion tea. Nobody in my family has had croup or catarrh for as long as I can remember."

Since older Southerners enjoy swapping complaints better than eating when they're hungry, you might have to come up with some grouses of your own to insinuate yourself further into their good graces. Bend your knees at a modest angle and ask if anyone has a remedy for cricks or night cramps. Then listen attentively and pour out profuse thanks when somebody suggests that you rub asafoetida on your calf or tie a snake's rattles on your left bedpost.

Throw in a few to-the-point questions, such as the efficacy of soaking in nettle water or wearing a copper anklet. Comment on your failure at getting slippery elm bark to do a thing for gout *or* warts. Throw cold water on the notion that bloodroot cures hunting hounds of sore pad or that bag balm helps chilblains. Give the impression that you may not know it all, but you're no rube at doctoring.

Outlook

The consummate bluffer should turn attention from negative thoughts and concentrate on what makes the average Southerner tick. To feign belonging in this august body, the bluffer needs an underlying sense of Southernness. That can come only from careful observation and duplication. Begin with your first contacts with the South and adapt your thinking as need be.

Take note that Dixie is the nation's vacationland, where an affinity for work is scarce as hens' teeth. From Myrtle Beach to Galveston, beaches abound. Join in the Chamber of Commerce spirit and support the natural wonders of dunes, sea oats, sandpipers, and warm breezes. Perk up your interest when the conversation turns to Pinehurst and golf courses. Let your eyes sparkle when you mention your own favorite getaway, be it a weekend at Kiawah or the Isle of Palms or a whole week of sternwheeling on the Big Muddy. Bluff along with any pastime. You don't need to mention details. Just emphasize R and R.

Observe that Southerners are inveterate optimists. Whatever the situation, they seem to make the best of it and come out on top. Even during the Great Depression, hillbillies staved off starvation in the same fashion they always did during hard times – by relying on farm produce for food and turning leftover grain into white lightning. The skill with which they eluded revenooers is legend, as recorded in Robert Mitchum's starring role in *Thunder Road.*

To express your allegiance to this point of view, lift your Mason jar high and swill a greasy draft of Appalachian moonshine with the good ole boys. Hide your discomfiture at the conflagration in your innards by demanding a hearty refill after that skimpy sip. Then, while the rest of the gathering dives into their cups, dispose of yours safely, away from heat and flame.

If you find yourself pressed into a third round, feign ulcers, irritable bowel, colitis, or religious principles. Limp a little and favor your hernia. Garner sympathy by reminding the gang that you fought for your country in Vietnam and have little capacity for spirits any more. Southerners are insanely patriotic. Have no fear—they'll think well of you.

Southerners are inveterate debaters, so get them off the subject of booze and onto something more cerebral. Initiate discussions of worthwhile topics, such as the reorganization of the Farm Bureau, the influx of Yankees to the Sun Belt, the Dixiecrats' chances in the primaries, Billy Graham's latest crusade among the heathens, recent vandalism at Graceland, or Richard Petty's abandonment of Plymouths in favor of Pontiacs. Very soon you'll note where sympathies lie. One thing about Southerners is certain—they're not shy about stating their views. As the discussion rises to fever pitch, lean back and absorb. Pretty soon you'll know which way to jump.

Profess a strong leaning toward Dixie's favorite toys—pickup trucks and RV's. Begin a match between Ford and Chevrolet fans, but don't let yourself be swept along on either side. If the exchange begins to produce more heat than light, sneer with conviction, "Well, neither one is going to have a chance if us red-blooded Americans don't stop buying trucks from them Japanese." Then mutter apprehensively about "watching our tail feathers for another sneak attack on Pearl Harbor" or mourn the sinking of the *Arizona*.

Speak favorably about home and hearth. Southerners may be violent, but they usually keep it in the family. Bluff your way through a discussion of Deep South homelife by vowing to fight for mother and apple pie, which in Dixie is served deep dish with ice cream. To edge away from muddy waters, drum up interest in a snack. Few Southerners can be diverted from their stomachs once someone brings up food.

The Southern Bias

To bolster your place among the in-crowd, try to see things as a Southerner sees them. First and foremost, no Yankee ever born can match a Dixieite in loyalty to old-time ways. Develop a hostile stir of hackles where anyone crowds your belief in the Old South. Speak out for rural values. Reject hot tubs and Jacuzzis, high-rises and condos. Call for a return to farm life at its best, Georgia style—not with a John Deere but a genuine jack and jenny.

Sneer irately at the Wall Street values of the great Northeast, particularly New York and its godless materialism. Throw in the loose-living Californians for good measure. Withhold judgment on the great in-between until all the evidence is gathered. For the time being, maintain allegiance to Dixie.

DEAR HEARTS AND GENTLE PEOPLE

At this point, you may be wondering if bluffing your way through the Deep South is worth it. It is. True, Southerners may seem snoopy at times, but it's not snoopiness as Yankees understand it. It's curiosity and concern. It means that you're "family." Your bluffing has paid off. Settle in and enjoy the best of the South. And the best, so far as most are concerned, is the genuine kindness and acceptance of its people. Southerners are known for many things—collards with cornbread and side meat, red clay soil and rutted side roads, late night skinny dipping and early morning rabbit hunts, *and* old schoolmates and asshole buddies. No self-respecting good ole boy would be without a passel of the latter. How would he pass a rainy Saturday, cheer Geoff, Richard, and Darryl at the Darlington 500, or weather a severe turn in his personal fortunes without someone to share it with? The very thought is ludicrous.

Thus, first off, learn nicknames. All true sons and daughters born below the Mason-Dixon Line retain standard names. For the men, James Lamar Dillingham IV, Thaddeus William Montgomery, Sr., or some similar arrangement of appellations, is fairly typical. Southern names are like fine monogrammed silver, prized fruitcake recipes, or heirloom spinning wheels—they never go out of the family. But only your mama or Great Aunt Effie would dare spit out so formal a concoction of names. Every Southern tad old enough to toddle is called Skip, Chip, Sonny, or Bubba. However idiotic the cognomen, brandish it at every opportunity.

For bluffing among women, the same situation abides. Women tend to bear double names, such as Mary Elizabeth or Wanda Sue or Evelyn Rose. Some carry their mother's maiden name in the middle, like Lynn Althea Conner Geitner or Bettina Renae Rawlings Mayfield. But these names last only through the christening. The test of old and endearing relationships is whether you are privy to a host of nicknames, like Babes or Lolly or T-Mama, dating to the morning Mrs. Oleta Mae Armbruster broke her left ulna and got a run in her stockings while trying to crank a dyspeptic T-model.

Once you've got the hang of the handles, do a lot of listening and sort everybody out. Figure out who of the gathering is cousin to whom and who is only a brother-in-law, factotum, or poor distant relative. Worm your way into the good graces of the group by cottoning to each person's special interests. If it's Cletus or Buster, emphasize huntin', fishin', and drinkin', all of which Buster decidedly prefers over his daily job of laying carpet—and Cletus, too, for that matter.

If it's Georgina, ask questions about last year's state fair. Cluck sympathetically when she tearfully discloses how unfair judging has become in the shortbread baking, granny square crocheting, or gladiolus growing contest. Mutter imprecations about politics taking over the world, even the kitchen and the garden.

To assure yourself a place among the best of chums, lean over and pull a bit of sweet grass or clover from the yard. Chew on the stem and spit occasionally over the rail (never indoors or at anybody's boots). Ease into a hand-woven split-bottomed oak slat chair, tip her back against the wall, and let one hand drop idly onto the head and ears of Otis's best bluetick, Big Red III. Say little and stroke a lot. Every Southerner trusts people who show a preference for dogs.

If the question of your birthplace brushes a little too close for comfort, interject questions about the trophy on the mantle under the portrait of Old Blue, who went to his reward during a quail hunt back in '49. Show genuine remorse for his demise, even if you have the urge to guffaw at the thought of an eighty-pound Airedale disappearing into a sinkhole without a trace. Ask if he left many offspring. Put your name on the list for the pick of the next litter. Insist that you mate Old Blue's great-great-great-grandson with your own Airedale bitch as soon as she comes in season.

Should you find yourself among womenfolk, weasel your way among the klatsch by absorbing the gossip and widening your eyes at appropriate revelations, such as a retelling of how Myrtle Mae Perry run off with that jakeleg itinerant preacher and how her papa hunted them down with his twelve gauge and hauled them both before the justice of the peace at two in the morning for a proper hitching. Snicker at the high spots of local dirty laundry, such as the birth of Rosa Fae Shook Hedgepath's twelve-and-a-half pound premature baby boy seven months after the wedding. This is easy bluffing and fun, too.

A remarkable thing may happen along your way to consummate bluffery. You may find yourself *so* warmly received among Southern folk that you never want to rejoin whatever lost tribe you originally sprang from. Quicker than a duck can peck a June bug, you too will have earned your own homespun handle and a regular place at the Thursday evening gatherings behind Joe Tillman's Amoco Service Center and Billiard Parlor. If I know the dear hearts and gentle people of my homeland, I wouldn't be a bit surprised.

GLOSSARY

The following list of terms includes words and phrases that often stump outsiders. With the proper guidance, bluffers can master these arcane bits of trivia and rise to the heights of bluffery.

ambrosia a holiday blend of fruit sections, shredded coconut, and rum or Southern Comfort. This colorful dessert is both tasty and hearty. Especially the gravy. Inexperienced bluffers have something to look forward to.

baroque seventeenth-century artistic style marked by grotesque or bizarre extravagances of design.

belvedere a gazebo or summer house. Many a sweet young thing has been deflowered in an unguarded moment whilst in the belvedere. Bluffers, take note.

Bible Belt a wide swath of the country peopled by fundamentalists and crackers (q.v.) of little or no education and a strong bent for superstition. Don't lock horns with the sterner members of this loosely defined geographic band.

bluegrass high-pitched harmony set to the picking and strumming of whatever stringed instruments lie at hand. Sessions are usually spontaneous and lively. Have no fear – this is not high-toned music.

booger tales down-home term for ghost stories or any tale or legend that terrifies the listener. Bluffers should practice up their skills before entering the fine old tradition of oral Southern literature.

bootjack a decorative, but functional, wrought-iron device that serves as a prop near entranceways or hearths for the removal of heavy boots.

carpetbagger any member of an unwelcome influx of Yankees, especially those who come to stay. Bluffers who blow their cover may be packing their carpetbags sooner than they expected.

catalpa worms fat green worms that are prized by anglers. (see night crawlers)

clodhopper an awkward, unrefined boob. Usually a figure of ridicule.

counterpane a bedspread or coverlet. In hillbilly terminology, this is referred to as a counterpin or coverlid.

cracker a disparaging, derogatory term for white, bigoted, violent Southerners, particularly in Georgia. Not to be confused with flat biscuits suitable for anchoring a smear of Peter Pan.

Dixie a name for the South derived from Daniel D. Emmett's minstrel classic (1859), which in turn derives from a slang name taken from the French word for *ten*, after a Louisiana ten-dollar bill. With all this derivating, smart bluffers will do well to question scholars. You never know when you can trust people with Ph.D.s.

Dixiecrat a Southern dissident who differs with

mainstream Democrats on civil rights issues. Easily confused with mossbacks (q.v.)

Dixieland jazz tunes played at double speed for a maximum rise in spirits. Often played very slowly on the way to the graveyard for Louisiana funerals; the tempo is heightened on the way back, usually because of the influence of booze.

footwashing Baptists an isolated group of fundamentalists (q.v.) who emulate the Mediterranean practice of washing the feet of fellow fundamentalists, particularly on Palm Sunday or Good Friday. These believers are not known for their openmindedness. (see below)

fundamentalist a deeply religious person who lacks education and who looks down on anyone who deviates even slightly from his or her narrowly formed creed.

gingerbread aside from the obvious, an architectural term that applies to wooden didoes and curlicues on Southern homes. For a thorough grounding, walk around the old section of Wilmington (North Carolina, not Delaware) or Savannah (Georgia, not Missouri).

grits soft fluffy mounds of cooked ground corn. Good with redeye (q. v.), cooked apples, and biscuits on a fall morning – or any morning, for that matter.

harmonium a simple version of a pump organ.

hillbilly a resident of isolated mountain coves who rejects refinement and clings to backwoods technology and beliefs. Usually, the term carries the connotion of poor and uneducated, but may be applied to people who relish their mountain origins in spite of public ridicule. Basically, they're "good country people."

hoppin' john a humble but hearty dish made from rice, dried peas, and pork.

jack and jenny male and female mules. There's more to be said about mule sexuality, but it requires more space than this small book. (Take my word for it—it's complicated.)

julep a syrupy, minty drink served in frosted silver cups and made from cracked ice, whiskey, sugar, and fresh-picked mint. It gets its name from the Persian words for rose water.

lagniappe a Creole-French term meaning "a little something extra."

lavabo an old-fashioned china washbowl that is sometimes accompanied by a pitcher.

live oak a nondeciduous oak tree of mammoth proportions that shades many parts of the South and provides a permanent dwelling for Spanish moss.

Mason-Dixon Line an eighteeth-century dividing line that settled a land dispute between the Calverts and the Penns. The term resurfaced in political history when Congress established the boundaries of the Missouri Compromise.

Mississippi mud pie a triple-layered chocolate pie that raises the blood sugar to steroid level.

Moon Pie a cookie and filling confection that consists of two pieces of shortbread, marshmallow cream center, and chocolate malt icing.

mossback an extremely tenacious oldtimer or reactionary. For a maximum understanding of this term, read any biography of Jesse Helms.

night crawlers juicy earthworms that lure perch and crappies to waiting hooks. Better than catfish dough for dock fishing.

no-see-'em a minuscule midge that can raise a mighty welt on exposed skin.

peckerwood no-count riff raff; undeserving of trust. If someone calls you this, take umbrage.

rebel yell (1) a blood-curdling screech which emulates the sound that Confederate troops made when going into battle; a Southern symbol of manhood. (2) a cheap brand of hooch.

redeye a slick, salty, brown-red gravy made by combining fresh-brewed coffee with ham grease left in the pan after country ham has been fried. (Honest, this is the real recipe.)

redneck a member of an almost indefinable belief system that glorifies violence and ignorance and flourishes among common laborers, millhands, and rural people in general. A redneck is a product of a complex combination of factors – rural influences and closed-mindedness (especially toward blacks, women, and non-rednecks). A redneck enjoys a frivolous lifestyle accompanied by alcoholic debauchery and has a fondness for hunting and male companionship at sporting events and a strong antipathy toward formality of dress and manners. At his worst (usually the term applies to males, but not irrevocably), his predilection for violence leads him to dangerous sports like Ku Klux Klan activities.

rococo lavish eighteenth-century ornamentation characterized by intricate decoration, especially by fancifully carved woodwork.

shagging a shuffling variation of the jitterbug that developed in the late 30s and rose to a peak of popularity along the Carolina coast during the late 50s and 60s. This dance is still enjoyed by baby boomers who want to relive their golden past.

sour mash a highly acidic grain mash (used in the distillation of whiskey) that has been exposed to yeast fermentation from a previous batch.

stereopticon a device used to view transparent slides that gives the impression of three-dimensional depth.

sweet bubby a common name for sweet shrub, a medium-sized plant that features a deep red anemone-shaped bud marked by a sweet fragrance.

unreconstructed an adjective referring to hardheads who want to go back to the plantation lifestyle of the antebellum South. Another name for these diehards is mossbacks (q.v.).

verandah uptown name for a porch. To Yankee yuppies, that's a deck with a top. (Wipe your feet. It may be outdoors, but it's a central family gathering place.)

White Camellia a white supremacist organization similar to but less lethal than the Ku Klux Klan. The less said about this era of Southern history the better.

white lightning crudely fermented sour mash whiskey made from corn and sugar, distilled through copper tubing, and decanted into homely containers, some of which are stoppered with rags or corncobs. A particular favorite of hillbillies.

white trash a white person who declines to live up to the standards of white society. Because Southern blacks are often unjustly relegated to a subhuman class, whites who sneer at propriety are labeled not merely trash but *white* trash. For example, women who smoke on the street are white trash. Likewise, whites who dump garbage by the roadside are white trash.

whup-ass an adjective suggesting a tendency toward fisticuffs, as in "Don't you take Almeda Louise to no Brass Rail Tavern. That's surely a whup-ass bar if I ever seen one. You know her mama is going to be bent outa shape if you escort a debutante to such trash as that."

whole hog an adverb meaning thoroughly or completely, as in "Almeda Louise may be a debutante, but she sure goes whole hog for a roll in the hay. Just don't let on to her mama I said so."

a whole nuther thang a phrase implying new or unknown territory, as in "Almeda Louise and I have been going together since high school, but marriage — well, sir! That's a *whole* nuther thang."

Bluffer's Guides
CENTENNIAL PRESS

The biggest bluff about the *Bluffer's Guides* is the title.
These books are full of information — and fun.

NOW IN STOCK — $3.95
Bluffer's Guide to Bluffing
Bluff Your Way in British Theatre
Bluff Your Way in Computers
Bluff Your Way in Hollywood
Bluff Your Way in Japan
Bluff Your Way in Management
Bluff Your Way in Music
Bluff Your Way in the Occult
Bluff Your Way in Paris
Bluff Your Way in Public Speaking

NEW TITLES
Bluff Your Way in Baseball
Bluff Your Way in the Deep South
Bluff Your Way in Football
Bluff Your Way in Golf
Bluff Your Way in Gourmet Cooking
Bluff Your Way in Marketing
Bluff Your Way in New York
Bluff Your Way in Wine

AVAILABLE SOON
Bluff Your Way in Basketball
Bluff Your Way in Office Politics
Bluff Your Way in Dining Out
Bluff Your Way in Fitness
Bluff Your Way in Home Maintenance
Bluff Your Way in Las Vegas
Bluff Your Way in London
Bluff Your Way in Marriage
Bluff Your Way in Parenting
Bluff Your Way in Psychology
Bluff Your Way in Sex

To order any of the Bluffer's Guides titles, use the order
form on the next page.

Get Bluffer's Guides at your bookstore or use this order form to send for the copies you want. Send it with your check or money order to:

Centennial Press
Box 82087
Lincoln, NE 68501

Title	Quantity	$3.95 Each
Total Enclosed		

Name_____

Address_____

City _____

State_____ Zip_____